AMY YOUNG

CONNECTED

STARTING YOUR
OVERSEAS LIFE
SPIRITUALLY FED

"But the fruit of the Spirit is love, joy, peace, patience, kindness, goodness, faithfulness, gentleness and self-control. Against such things there is no law."

Galatians 5:22-23, ESV

Contents

Introduction

Banquets are an integral part of life in China and have layers of rules that can make it stressful for an outsider. While banquets where I grew up were always formal, in China they can be formal (and expensive to host), or informal at a local restaurant or in your home (still expensive to host). Part of the stress of banquets at the beginning of my time in China were all of the unknowns: Where should I sit? Do I have to eat that food that was just placed in my bowl? If so, do I have to eat all of it, or will a "thank you" nibble suffice? When am I supposed to make my toast? What should I say?! How much should I eat? You can see why it was stressful for a newbie!

At the first banquet I attended, early into the event I wondered, "Why are others eating so little?" as I ate my regular sized portions. But as food kept coming out and I became so full I thought I might throw up if I kept eating, I realized that everyone else knew to pace their eating throughout the meal. Over time, as I learned the rules and understood the role of banquets and how to feed myself, I grew to love them.

Learning how to feed yourself on the field is no small feat and will take more time than you ever imagined. Ironically, spiritual feeding on the field will also take time to adjust to. Your new context is different and it takes time to figure out what works, what doesn't work at all, and what you need to adapt in order to be spiritually fed. The sermons, books, and podcasts you brought to the field to feed your soul and relationship with God may not work as you hoped. Examples that resonate with a North American audience seem almost ridiculous when heard or read in your new context. For example, I didn't have running hot water in my first apartment on the field. The hot water pipes in my apartment were broken during a repair and it was too hard to fix them. So, the one hour a day we had hot water in my teammate's apartment, we took turns who would shower in her bathroom first. You should have seen how excited we around 9 p.m. every evening when water started to gush through the pipes in her apartment, rattling the walls. None of the sermons I had brought with me mentioned excitement at hearing the pipes rattle with your one hour of running hot water. Instead they referenced minivans, Target stores, and other parts of culture that couldn't be further from my life.

In sharing this example, I don't want you to feel despondent that you might never connect with a sermon or book "from home" again. What I do want you to know is that if you are feeling this way or start to feel this way at a point in the future, know it won't last forever. Over time, as you move through the adjusting phase, sermons and other resources can feed you again. It's just that at the beginning the gap between your new reality and the examples given in sermons and books may be too great and might not help to your soul or nurture your relationship with God. And that's okay.

Sometimes it's good to set certain resources aside for a season and focus on something else. In this case, focusing on the fruit of the spirit mentioned in Galatians 5:22-23. As I studied the fruit of the spirit for my book *Getting Started: Making the Most of Your First Year in Cross-Cultural Service*, it seemed that the order of the fruit is uniquely arranged for your adjustment to the field and bonding to your new cultures. I could only touch on the fruit of the spirit briefly in *Getting Started,* and hope that this additional resource will feed your soul and nurture your relationship with God as you adjust to cross-cultural life.

Over the course of this book, and for simplicity when so much of life is new, each month you will focus on one fruit listed in the Galatians passage, one verse or short passage, and a set of seven questions for reflection. If you are reading this electronically, you might want to use a notebook to record your answers. If you are reading a physical copy of this book, I left you space to write your reflections. Either way, once a week pull out the questions for that month and spend time cultivating the fruit for that month. May God meet you in these pages as He goes before you, behind you, and besides you.

Love

Love truly covers a multitude of sins and annoyances (1 Peter 4:8). If you have the foundation of love for the culture you are making home, the local people you interact with, and your teammates, you will be able to weather the tough days when they come.

VERSES:

"And so we know and rely on the love God has for us. God is love. Whoever lives in love lives in God, and God in them. This is how love is made complete among us so that we will have confidence on the day of judgment: In this world we are like Jesus. There is no fear in love. But perfect love drives out fear, because fear has to do with punishment. The one who fears is not made perfect in love. We love because he first loved us." 1 John 4:16–19

SUGGESTIONS AND QUESTIONS
FOR REFLECTION:

1. Copy the verse below and interact with it in some way. For instance, you could draw a picture, write your thoughts, or circle/underline words. Also, put the verse somewhere you can see—your screen saver, in the bathroom, or in the kitchen—so that you can meditate on it during the month.

2. Every day record one thing you loved about the day (or the previous day if you are writing them down in the morning).

3. What new sounds, smells, and tastes did you hear, smell, or try this month?

4. Learn something about your teammate(s) throughout the month. For some, this will be easy, for others you will need to be intentional.

5. If you are in the honeymoon phase, enjoy it! Write down what you love, take pictures, and try to capture snippets of what you love. If you skipped the honeymoon and instead had a crash landing, remember that love is not always a feeling, sometimes it is a decision. While you admit this is fill-in-the-blank _________________ (disappointing/frustrating/scary/confusing), write down what you hope to come to love about your new home.

6. What has God shown you about love this month?

7. What would it look like for you to love your life and calling in this place?

Joy

Your bags are likely (mostly) unpacked and daily life is starting to become more manageable. Can you believe you are here?! After so much praying, dreaming, filling out of forms, support raising, preparing, and traveling, this is now your life. As you meditate on this month's verse, picture God rejoicing over you in song. He is delighted when He sees you trying a new food, practicing a new word, opening yourself to a new experience. Building on the foundation of love for *this* land and *these* people, in month two you will focus on joy.

VERSE:

"The Lord your God is with you, the Mighty Warrior who saves. He will take great delight in you; in his love he will no longer rebuke you, but will rejoice over you with singing." Zephaniah 3:17

SUGGESTIONS AND QUESTIONS
FOR REFLECTION:

1. Copy the verse below and interact with it in some way. For instance, you could draw a picture, write your thoughts, or circle/underline words. Also, put the verse somewhere you can see—your screen saver, in the bathroom, or in the kitchen—so that you can meditate on it during the month.

2. What delights you about this culture? These people? Your team?

3. What parts of the culture or your team have been harder than you expected?

4. In those hard places, what might God be showing you about joy?

5. Where have you sensed God's joy this month?

6. What has God shown you about joy this month?

7. Where have you sensed God rejoicing over you? How do you know God delights in you?

Peace

As the newness of your time here on the field begins to rub off and you see another side of your current culture, local people, and teammates, it's easy to feel anxious and a desire to put blinders on and hide. Instead of blinders, what you need is peace. In Hebrew, peace is defined as "peace, wholeness, completeness, fulfillment, security, harmony, well-being, and contentment."[1] These are the things that you need. Building on love and joy, this month you will focus on peace.

VERSE:

"And the peace of God, which transcends all understanding, will guard your hearts and your minds in Christ Jesus." Philippians 4:7

---

1 Danielle Wheeler, "I Just Want Peace," *Velvet Ashes*, April 24, 2019, https://velvetashes.com/i-just-want-peace.

SUGGESTIONS AND QUESTIONS
FOR REFLECTION:

1. Copy the verse below and interact with it in some way. For instance, you could draw a picture, write your thoughts, or circle/underline words. Also, put the verse somewhere you can see—your screen saver, in the bathroom, or in the kitchen—so that you can meditate on it during the month.

2. Where do you feel peaceful in your new culture?

3. Where do you feel anxious or stirred up? How would peace make a difference?

4. What parts of the culture or local people need God's peace? As you are still new, what do you need to understand more about a situation? Who could you ask about it?

5. Which comes most naturally to you: love, joy, or peace.
How has that fruit enhanced your first three months?

6. What did God show you about His peace this month?

7. How have you come to experience and see peace in a new
way this month?

Patience

Patience could not come at a better time! In my fourth month on the field, I was colder than I had ever been in my life . . . and knew I still had months to go before I would genuinely be warm outside of my bed. Maybe where you are you are hot, hot, hot! Or maybe you are cold, cold, cold. Perhaps you are longing for the weather to change after months of sameness, or you are wanting to learn the language faster, or wondering why your friends back home seem to have forgotten you. Enter stage left: patience. This month you will add patience to the love you are tending for the land and people, the joy of being God's child, and peace that brings wholeness.

VERSE:

"Whoever is patient has great understanding, but one who is quick-tempered displays folly." Proverbs 4:29

SUGGESTIONS AND QUESTIONS
FOR REFLECTION:

1. Copy the verse below and interact with it in some way. For instance, you could draw a picture, write your thoughts, or circle/underline words. Also, put the verse somewhere you can see—your screen saver, in the bathroom, or in the kitchen—so that you can meditate on it during the month.

2. Right now, this very day, where do you need patience?

3. Are you finding it easier or more challenging to be patient compared to your first month here? What is God showing you about yourself when it comes to patience? What is God teaching you about Himself when it comes to patience?

4. Are you finding it easier or more challenging to be patient than in your "home" country?

5. When you consider the work that you have come to be a part of, where will you need to be more patient than you anticipated?

6. Where have you seen God be patient with you?

7. What did God show you about patience this month?

Kindness

Kindness is underrated in our world. I believe that if your time on the field is flavored with kindness, you will do more for the kingdom of God than if you have the best strategies or technology or whatever else you think you might need to be successful. But, here's the rub with kindness—it is slow and small. By month five you might be chomping at the bit to see something big and grand happen for God. "Come on," you think, "It's been five months! Where is the action?!" Focusing on kindness for a month is the perfect antidote to these thoughts. This month you will add kindness to the foundation of love, as you continue to delight in aspects of your life (joy), experience God's shalom (peace), and allow God to work in His timing (patience).

VERSE:

"Be kind and compassionate to one another, forgiving each other, just as in Christ God forgave you." Ephesians 4:32

SUGGESTIONS AND QUESTIONS FOR REFLECTION:

1. Copy the verse below and interact with it in some way. For instance, you could draw a picture, write your thoughts, or circle/underline words. Also, put the verse somewhere you can see—your screen saver, in the bathroom, or in the kitchen—so that you can meditate on it during the month.

2. Keep a daily record this month of kindness extended to you.

3. In the past four months, recall a kindness a local friend, teammate, and supporter extended to you. How did God meet you in each kind act?

4. Kindness is often small and slow on the field. How does this truth help counterbalance the pull for big and grand? Where have you enjoyed the small and slow?

5. Who could you be kind to today?

57

6. Where have you seen God be kind with you?

7. What has God shown you about kindness this month?

Goodness

You are half-way through your first year, can you believe it? My friend Joann Pittman says that solid theology is like a three-legged stool holding these three truths: God is good, God is sovereign, and life is hard. If you remove any one of the legs, the stool falls over. Maybe you are still deeply aware of God's goodness as your time on the field so far has been fantastic and this will be a month of celebration. Or maybe it's been the opposite of fantastic. Maybe you are wondering about your call and if you heard God wrong. If so, this month can recalibrate the "God is good" leg of your stool. For five months you have built upon the foundation of love, joy, peace, patience, and kindness, trying to see each fruit in your new culture, locals, and team. Now you'll focus on God's goodness in this place and time, wherever you may find yourself.

VERSE:

"Let us not become weary in doing good, for at the proper time we will reap a harvest if we do not give up." Galatians 6:9

SUGGESTIONS AND QUESTIONS
FOR REFLECTION:

1. Copy the verse below and interact with it in some way. For instance, you could draw a picture, write your thoughts, or circle/underline words. Also, put the verse somewhere you can see—your screen saver, in the bathroom, or in the kitchen—so that you can meditate on it during the month.

2. God's goodness is universal. Where have you seen it in action in the culture? In nature where you live? In the food, music, dancing, or other forms of expression?

3. God's goodness is also personal. Psalm 34:8 says, "Taste and see that the Lord is good." Where have you tasted the Lord's goodness to you since you arrived? Where have you tasted it this month?

4. What good works has God called you to be a part of? How has the work you are doing—even if it does not seem directly related to the work, like language learning or schooling your children—participated in God's goodness?

5. How receptive have locals been to the good you are doing (or want to do)? How has their openness or closedness impacted you?

6. What about life here drains you and makes doing good hard for you? Be honest with God as you reflect; He wants to meet you in those hard places.

7. What has God shown you about goodness this month?

Faithfulness

Here you are, month seven! This is a perfect time in our journey to focus on faithfulness. Faithfulness is built slowly over time and often is invisible at first glance. Even so, faithfulness does the vital work of holding a body together, just like tendons and sinews. Tendons are not the exciting, easy to see parts of the body; but a case of tendonitis in the wrists or elbows (and I've been there!) points to the truth that the whole body suffers when they're not right. If you love where you are and what you are doing, are able to live with delight, experience God's peace, grow in patience, are kind to those you interact with daily, note God's goodness where you are, but are unfaithful . . . people won't trust you. Thankfully, faithfulness is yours with God's help.

VERSE:

"Lord, you are my God; I will exalt you and praise your name, for in perfect faithfulness you have done wonderful things, things planned long ago." Isaiah 25:1

SUGGESTIONS AND QUESTIONS
FOR REFLECTION:

1. Copy the verse below and interact with it in some way. For instance, you could draw a picture, write your thoughts, or circle/underline words. Also, put the verse somewhere you can see—your screen saver, in the bathroom, or in the kitchen—so that you can meditate on it during the month.

2. Often in Christian circles we associate faithfulness with a marriage relationship. Yet, we are all called to be faithful in every stage of life, whether we are six or eighty-two years old. What does it look like for you to be faithful to the culture you live in? What does faithfulness look like as you interact with locals and with your team?

3. Reflecting on your first six months, where were you unfaithful to the culture, to local friends, and to teammates? If you're not sure, scan your memory and look for places in your thoughts or in a private email to a friend that you wrote something you hope is never read more broadly. Where were you faithful even when it was hard?

4. What makes it challenging to be faithful in this context? For example, maybe corruption is a problem, or you find yourself competing with others in language school, or supporters have not been loyal in fulfilling a commitment they made to you.

5. Where have you seen God's faithfulness to you?

6. Look back on the six other fruits of the spirit. How does faithfulness relate to love, joy, peace, patience, kindness, and goodness in your current context?

7. What have you learned about faithfulness this month?

Gentleness

Gentleness might seem to fit better with peace and joy than sandwiched here between faithfulness and self-control. Be that as it may, it's perfectly placed for your journey. Month eight is about the time you need to be reminded to be gentle with yourself, with your family, and with your team. Maybe the work you were chomping at the bit to get to in months one and two is moving at a sloth's pace and it's killing you. Instead of focusing on how to get things going or try to add some fuel to the fire, God knows that if your zeal (or frustration) is not tempered with gentleness, you will come across like a clanging gong or fingernails on a chalkboard. As you have grown in love, joy, peace, patience, kindness, goodness, and faithfulness towards your host culture, local friends, and teammates, now let's look at learning to live with a gentle spirit.

VERSE:

"Let your gentleness be evident to all. The Lord is near."
Philippians 4:5

SUGGESTIONS AND QUESTIONS FOR REFLECTION:

1. Copy the verse below and interact with it in some way. For instance, you could draw a picture, write your thoughts, or circle/underline words. Also, put the verse somewhere you can see—your screen saver, in the bathroom, or in the kitchen—so that you can meditate on it during the month.

2. Are you drawn to gentleness? Who in your life is gentle? What draws you to that person?

3. What does it look like to be a gentle man in your "home" and host culture? What does it look like to be a gentle woman in your "home" and host culture? When is gentleness shown in your host culture?

4. How was God gentle with you as you prepared for the field? How has He been gentle to you in your first seven months here?

5. In both Greek and Hebrew gentleness is related to not doing harm and being humble.[2] Considering the culture and your interactions with locals and teammates, where or with whom do you need to cultivate more gentleness?

---

2 "What is gentleness?" *Spirit Home,* http://www.spirithome.com/gentleness.html.

6. Who has been gentle with you recently? Ask the Holy Spirit to bring gentle gestures, comments, and actions of someone or others to mind.

7. What have you learned about gentleness this month?

89

Self-Control

In His kindness towards you, God did not start this journey of adjusting to your new culture with you needing to focus on self-control; instead, He invited you to start building a foundation of love. Now, nine months in, He is introducing the idea of restraint. Why so long? Because, ironically, you've now been here long enough to be dangerous to yourself and others. You no longer have to ask for help as much as you did; you know your way around; you have routines and friends; daily life is manageable (even if parts are exhausting). But you also have much to learn. Amen? Amen. Being able to harness your energies and assert your power over your reactions, thoughts, and desires is possible with God's help. As you build upon your love for this place, the locals, and your team, live with delight, experience God's peace, grow in patience, are kind to those you interact with daily, note God's goodness where you are, are faithful in word and deed, and have humble gentleness, God is inviting you into greater self-control.

VERSE:

"Like a city whose walls are broken through is a person who lacks self-control." Proverbs 25:28

SUGGESTIONS AND QUESTIONS
FOR REFLECTION:

1. Copy the verse below and interact with it in some way. For instance, you could draw a picture, write your thoughts, or circle/underline words. Also, put the verse somewhere you can see—your screen saver, in the bathroom, or in the kitchen—so that you can meditate on it during the month.

2. Where has self-control been more effortless for you here than back "home"? Where has it been more challenging?

3. Maybe language studies are not going as fast as you would like. Maybe doors you thought would open have been slow to open or haven't budged. Maybe your team relations are not as deep as you would like. How is God meeting you in your desire to move more quickly?

4. Where have you extended self-control towards others recently? Where do you think others have shown self-control when interacting with you?

5. Paul compares self-control to the physical training an athlete does (1 Corinthians 9). What spiritual practices and rhythms have helped you these past eight months? Are there any routines that haven't been as meaningful in this first year on the field as they were before?

6. Look back over the eight other fruit of the spirit. How does self-control relate to love, joy, peace, patience, kindness, goodness, faithfulness, and gentleness in your current context?

7. What have you learned about self-control this month?

Conclusion

Here we are at the end of your first nine months. Isn't it a bit uncanny how the fruit of the spirit line up with the adjustments you have experienced these first nine months? When Paul wrote his letter to the Galatians he was frustrated; in trying to figure out what to keep and what to discard from the law, the Galatians kept more than they discarded, remaining more in bondage than they needed to be. Though Paul had to say it repeatedly to the Galatians, he never tired of reminding them—and us—that a life in the Spirit is marked by freedom. My hope and prayer is that these nine months have pointed you to the One who offers freedom, not only to those you came to serve, but to you as well. Truly, these nine months have been pivotal. Hopefully you have tasted the freedom in Christ you can experience here in your new surroundings—your new home. A freedom marked by love, joy, peace, patience, kindness, goodness, faithfulness, gentleness and self-control. May the Lord bless you and keep you, and may all the days on the field—whether few or many—be marked by the fruit of the Spirit.

Acknowledgments

I love reading acknowledgments and learning more of the behind-the-scenes on a book.

Connected was born through *Getting Started* being too long. I needed to eliminated 6,000 words and texted my friend and fellow writer Leslie Verner to hold me accountable and with a bit too much glee (from my sad perspective) was all in.

Some editing is like trimming nails, other is like removing limbs. But if the limbs are meant to be, they will go on to find another place to live. Thank you, Leslie, for encouraging the chopping.

Because writing is a solitary activity, in my case done mostly at the public library, in the basement, on the back deck, I am grateful for the writing communities that cheer me on, hold me accountable, and understand that showing up day after day is the real work of genius. Thank you to David Rupert and *The Writers on the Rock* community in Colorado. Thank you *KB Mastermind Group*, we might be small, but our hour-long skype calls every two weeks do more to keep me accountable to my goals than anything else I do. Britta, Esther, and Kathy, I love you and a million thanks.

Books do not happen without many investing their time, talents, and wisdom. Thank you, Stacey Covell, for editing and Vanessa Mendozzi for the cover and layout design work. The Global Trellis team pushes me to do and be better for cross-cultural workers and I love working with you! My friends and family remind me that most of life is lived off the page. I love you Mom, Dad, Elizabeth, Laura, Del, Sue, Emily, Katy, Anna, and Chloe.

Dear reader, I am also grateful you are here. Thank you for buying *Connected*, could I ask one more favor? A simple yet meaningful way to help an author is to leave a review on Amazon or Goodreads (it does not need to be five stars, any review helps). Thank you for buying and reading this small offering to life on the field.

About Amy

Amy Young is a writer, speaker, and advocate for embracing the messy middle in life. After nearly twenty years in China, she cofounded the online community Velvet Ashes. She also founded Global Trellis an online space for personal, professional, and spiritual development of cross-cultural workers. She enjoys cheering for the Denver Broncos, the Kansas Jayhawks, and libraries. Though she misses steaming dumplings in Beijing, Amy currently lives in Denver, Colorado and, much to her surprise, enjoys gardening.